Magic M

Contents	Page
Source of Maple Syrup	2
First producers	4
Early history	6
Discovery legends	8-11
Early harvesting methods	12-13
Concentration methods	14
Teaching the process	16-17
Harvesting	18-19
Products	20-21
Treats and celebration	22
Index	24

written by Pam Holden

maple trees

If you have tasted maple syrup you already know that it is delicious to enjoy poured over pancakes, waffles, ice cream, oatmeal and other food. You know that it's a sweet, sticky treat, but are you aware that it comes from the sap of a tree?
It is obtained from 3 types of maple tree:
red, black, and sugar maple.
These remarkable trees are grown on sugar farms in cold climate areas of Canada and the United States. They live for 200-300 years, reaching enormous heights.

People have been enjoying maple syrup for hundreds of years. The native people of North America were the first to produce maple syrup and maple sugar long before settlers arrived from Europe several hundred years ago. The earliest written records were made by European explorers in the 1600s. The pioneers who followed were keen to trade goods for the sugary products.

early traders

No one really knows how the Native Americans learned to make their delicious "sweet water", which was totally unknown anywhere else in the world. Each tribe still has its own legend to describe their discovery of the amazing secret of the maple tree. These stories have been told countless times to many generations.

7

One likely legend tells how a man observed a squirrel drinking from a branch it had bitten. He wondered why it was not drinking fresh water from the thawing lake nearby. Puzzled, he broke a branch and watched a tiny stream of clear, watery sap trickle down the trunk.
When he gently touched his finger on the sap and licked it, he was surprised to find it tasted sweet and delicious! He placed a small wooden bowl below the stream of sap to catch the precious drops. At daybreak the next morning he hurried back to check his bowl. To his delight he found enough sap to take home proudly to his family. Everyone loved the wonderful new drink they named "sweet water". They quickly learned successful ways to harvest and use the sap every spring.

Another legend tells about an old woman who trudged to a maple tree to collect a wooden bucketful of sap. When she returned to her tepee she tipped the sap into an earthenware cooking pot, which she hung over her fire to warm. Feeling exhausted after walking and carrying the heavy bucket home, she lay down for a short rest, but fell sound asleep. When she awoke several hours later, she hurried to check the cooking pot and was astonished to find a sweet thick syrup had developed from the sap.

Some say that by chance a sharp tomahawk lodged in a tree trunk released sap into a bucket left below the tree. A woman who found it mistook the liquid for water, so she took it home and cooked food in it. Her delighted family declared it was delicious, asking eager questions about where it had been discovered, and how they could find more.

People of the Alonquin tribe named the sap "sinzibuckwud", which means "drawn from wood". They used tomahawks to make V-shaped cuts in the trunks of maple trees, then poked in reeds or curved bark pieces – this let the sap gradually run down into wooden bowls or buckets.

These containers had to be carefully carried back to their settlement, where the sap was changed to syrup. Sap contains an extremely high proportion of water, which must be evaporated to reduce the liquid to a thick syrup. It takes forty buckets of sap to produce one single bucket of maple syrup!

concentrating the sap

Three methods were used to concentrate the sap:
1. By dropping red-hot cooking stones from the fire directly into a bucketful of sap, causing the water to come off as steam, condensing the liquid.
2. By leaving a bucketful of sap outdoors to freeze solid overnight, then removing the thick layer of ice which had formed on top.
3. By boiling the sap for several hours in earthenware pots over a steady wood fire protected by a roof of branches.

The resulting syrup was used as a sweet drink or in cooking, and as a medicine.

The Native American people demonstrated this time-consuming process to arriving European settlers, who were keen to learn the steps of the harvest and production of "sweet water". They learned how to tap the trunks of maple trees at the beginning of spring, collect the sap in buckets, and boil it to evaporate most of the water.

The Native Americans also shared their special secrets of sugar-making, showing how even more water could be boiled out of the syrup to produce maple sugar. This became popular and widely-used, as other kinds of sugar were expensive and hard to obtain.

tapping a maple tree

The harvesting season lasts only a few weeks in early spring, before the trees begin to sprout buds. After being frozen all winter, the sap begins to thaw. Trees are "tapped" by drilling two or three holes into the trunks to release the sap, which dribbles down into buckets or plastic bags or tubes.

Early settlers used horse-drawn sleds to collect buckets of sap every single day during the short harvesting season. These were taken to a sugar shed to be emptied into vats for boiling.

In later years, tractors and wagons were used for the daily collection and transport of buckets. Nowadays modern methods of production have been developed. Plastic tubes are fitted to cuts drilled in the trees to carry sap directly to vats in the processing plant for evaporation.

Some of the syrup is boiled even further to produce maple cream or butter, maple sugar and toffee. Sap must be handled carefully and filtered to make sure the distilled syrup is totally natural and pure. Nothing must be added.

Be aware that there are some imitation products available on the market – usually marked "Maple-flavored". Producers of pure maple syrup joke that imitation syrup is made by tapping telephone poles instead of maple trees!

pure maple syrup

sugar on snow

"Sugar on snow" is a traditional springtime treat made by pouring hot, freshly-made maple syrup over clean snow. It suddenly turns waxy and is eaten like candy – delicious! Festivals are held each spring wherever maple syrup is produced to celebrate this wonderful treat from the trees. Thousands of people visit sugar farms where they can learn its history and observe how it is produced. Tractor wagons take visitors on sugar bush tours. At pancake barns they enjoy maple syrup served many ways, and some people buy a supply to take home – enough to last until next spring!
Try magic maple syrup for yourself!

Index   **Page**

Index	Page
festivals	22
harvest	18-19
imitation syrup	20
legends	6, 8, 10
Native Americans	4-13, 16-17
sap	2, 8-10, 12-13, 16, 18, 20
settlers	4, 16, 18
squirrel	8
trees	2, 18
treats	2, 20, 22